WOMAN TO WOMAN
VIRTUAL OR VIRTUOUS
WHO ARE YOU?

DR. KATRINA EDWARDS

WOMAN TO WOMAN
VIRTUAL OR VIRTUOUS

WHO ARE YOU?

Published by Krystal Lee Enterprises (KLE Publishing)
Copyright © 2025 by Katrina Edwards. All rights re-
served. Please send comments and questions:

Krystal Lee Enterprises
770-240-0089 Ext. 1
sales@KLEPub.com

To Reach the Author:
Email: virtuenwomen@gmail.com

Cover Design: Rayven Baker - ImageRé

ISBN: **979-8-89987-909-8**
E-book: 979-8-89987-910-4

Acknowledgements

I would like to begin by dedicating this book to my Lord and Savior, Jesus Christ. His grace, wisdom, and unwavering presence have guided me through every step of this journey.

To my husband, John, your steadfast support, patience, and love have been my anchor throughout the writing of this book. I am deeply grateful for your encouragement and belief in me.

To Chris, Johnathan, Joshua, and James, thank you for continually seeing my full potential and trusting the process. Your confidence in me has been both motivating and humbling.

To my mother, the first virtuous woman I ever knew and cherished. Your prayers, wisdom, and unwavering love have carried me through every season of life. From my earliest days until now, your guidance has been godly, your counsel full of wisdom, and your love steadfast. You have demonstrated and lived the proverbs 31 woman. Thank you, Mom.

To Sabrina, my sister who deserves God's very best. You have persevered through life's challenges and shown a resilience that inspires everyone around you. Your strength is quiet but unshakable, your faith steady even in uncertainty, and your heart remains open despite all you've faced. Thank you for being a living reminder that courage is not the absence of struggle, but the grace with which we continue forward. I honor you, I admire you, and I pray that every blessing you've poured into others returns to you a hundredfold.

To Toni, thank you for being my constant sounding board and trusted voice of reason on every project. Your insight and encouragement have been invaluable.

And to Rayven, thank you for always understanding my vision and bringing it to life so beautifully. You consistently capture exactly what I imagine for the book cover design.

WOMAN TO WOMAN
VIRTUAL OR VIRTUOUS
WHO ARE YOU?

Table of Contents

Dr. Katrina Edwards

Introduction

In today's world, women face many challenges as they strive to balance the demands of modern life with traditional expectations of femininity and morality. At the heart of this struggle is the question of what it means to be a virtuous woman, and how this concept has evolved over time. In this book, we will explore the characteristics and differences between a virtuous woman and a virtual woman, in an effort to gain a deeper understanding of what it means to be a good woman in the 21st Century.

The idea of the "virtuous woman" is deeply rooted in cultural, spiritual, and historical frameworks. From ancient religious texts to philosophical writings, the virtuous woman has long been upheld as an ideal—often characterized by qualities such as integrity, humility, loyalty, wisdom, compassion, and strength. In many societies, she has been seen as the moral compass of the family, the keeper of values, and the foundation upon which strong communities are built.

Introduction

Yet, as the digital age rapidly reshapes our lives, another archetype has emerged: the "virtual woman." Unlike the traditional notion of virtue, the virtual woman is shaped by technology, media, and online culture. She is often curated through screens, filters, algorithms, and likes. Her identity is fluid, ever-evolving, and heavily influenced by societal trends, digital platforms, and public opinion. While the virtual woman may be empowered, visible, and even celebrated, she is also vulnerable to being objectified, commodified, and misunderstood.

This dichotomy between the virtuous and the virtual creates a tension that many modern women feel deeply. On one hand, there is the desire to honor timeless principles, to live with purpose and moral clarity, and to cultivate inner character. On the other hand, there is a pressure to remain relevant, to succeed in a hyper-connected world, and to meet external standards of beauty, performance, and identity. For many, the lines between these two ideals blur, and the challenge becomes not just how to choose between them, but how to reconcile them.

In this book, we seek to unpack this complex conversation. What does it really mean to be a "virtuous woman" today? Can virtue coexist with visibility? Can tradition be preserved without suppressing progress? How do women navigate their personal values in a world that often prizes appearance over authenticity, immediacy over introspection, and influence over integrity?

To answer these questions, we will examine a wide range of perspectives: historical and religious teachings, modern-day feminism, psychological studies, and real-life stories from women of diverse backgrounds. We will look at how technology has transformed the way women see themselves and are seen by others, and what that means for their self-worth, relationships, careers, and spiritual lives.

The concept of the "virtual woman" will also be carefully explored. She is not inherently negative or shallow. In fact, the virtual space can be a powerful tool for women to express themselves, advocate for change, and build communities. However, we must also acknowledge the risks that come with a digital existence, such as disconnection from one's true self, the rise of performative identity, and the erosion of private and sacred values. When virtual living replaces real connection and inner growth, the cost can be high.

Moreover, this book does not aim to shame or divide women into rigid categories. Rather, it seeks to open a conversation about the values we hold dear and the lives we choose to lead. It invites readers to reflect deeply: Who are we becoming in the process of chasing modern success? What are we sacrificing in the name of progress? How do we define our worth—and by whose standards?

Introduction

Ultimately, this is a call to return to something deeper: A sense of identity that is grounded in character rather than image, in purpose rather than popularity, and in truth rather than trend. It is about rediscovering the beauty and strength of virtuous living, not as an outdated ideal, but as a timeless foundation for a fulfilled, meaningful life.

The virtuous woman of today may not look exactly like the one described in ancient texts, but her essence remains the same. She is intentional. She is courageous. She is generous, wise, and resilient. She is not perfect, but she strives to live with integrity. She is not invisible, but she is not defined by visibility. And most importantly, she is free not in the sense of doing whatever she wants, but in the deeper sense of living in alignment with who she truly is and who God has created her to be.

As we journey through the chapters ahead, we will dive deeper into these ideas and explore what it truly means to be a virtuous woman in a virtual age. We will look at real-life challenges in relationships, career, motherhood, identity, and faith to see how virtue can guide us through them. We will reflect on how every woman, regardless of her background or beliefs, can reclaim her value in a world that often confuses visibility with worth.

This is not just a book about women. It is a book for anyone seeking clarity, authenticity, and purpose in an age of noise and distraction. The future belongs not just to the visible, but to the virtuous.

Let's begin.

Chapter 1

The Virtuous Woman

Proverbs 31:10 "Who can find a virtuous woman? For her price is far above rubies."

The concept of a virtuous woman has been a part of human culture for thousands of years and has been celebrated and revered in literature, religion, and philosophy. A virtuous woman is often seen as a model of moral and ethical behavior, embodying qualities such as kindness, compassion, honesty, and selflessness. In many cultures, the virtuous woman is also seen as a symbol of strength and resilience, able to withstand the challenges of life with grace and dignity.

But who, exactly, is this virtuous woman, and why has her image endured through the centuries?

From the ancient world to modern times, the idea of virtue has always been tied to character. It is not about perfection or appearance, but about inward strength, moral consistency, and the ability to live according to one's deepest values. A virtuous woman does not merely *appear* good—she *is* good, even when no one is watching.

One of the most famous portrayals of the virtuous woman is found in the Hebrew Bible, in the Book of Proverbs, Chapter 31. This passage paints a portrait of a woman who is industrious, wise, generous, and God fearing. She rises early, provides for her household, speaks with wisdom, and is praised not for her beauty, but for her character: *"Charm is deceptive, and beauty is fleeting; but a woman who fears the Lord is to be praised"* (Proverbs 31:30).

This depiction is not simply a checklist of duties; it is a celebration of womanhood rooted in purpose, diligence, and reverence. The virtuous woman is strong but not hardened. She is tender, but not weak. She is confident, but not boastful. Her power lies not in dominance, but in devotion to her values, her family, her faith, and her community.

In ancient Greece, philosophers like Aristotle also linked virtue to the idea of living in accordance with reason and moral excellence. While much of their discussion centered around men, the concept of the virtuous life was seen as the highest aim for any human being. A virtuous woman, then, was one who practiced moderation, wisdom, justice, and courage not just in public, but within the private sphere of family and relationships.

In Eastern traditions, such as Confucianism, the ideal woman was expected to uphold the values of loyalty, humility, and respect within the family structure. Though these expectations were often restrictive, they also reflected a deep recognition of a woman's role as a stabilizing force within society. The virtuous woman was not passive; she was essentially a quiet yet powerful presence shaping the moral fabric of the next generation.

What is striking across cultures and eras is that the virtuous woman is rarely defined by what she owns, how she looks, or how loudly she speaks. Instead, she is defined by how she lives by the integrity of her actions, the consistency of her principles, and the kindness of her spirit. In every age, she has been a source of hope and healing, a pillar of strength when everything else seems to fall apart.

Today, however, the virtues that once defined womanhood are often overshadowed by the pressures of modern performance culture. Success is measured by speed, visibility, and external achievement. As a result, the inner life where true virtue is cultivated is frequently neglected.

But this does not mean that virtue is outdated. On the contrary, it is more needed than ever.

In a world flooded with noise, a virtuous woman is one who listens before she speaks. In a culture obsessed with image, she chooses integrity over impression. In an age of instant gratification, she practices patience, knowing that lasting fruit comes from deep roots.

Virtue today may look different from it did centuries ago, but its essence remains. It might look like a mother working two jobs to provide for her children with dignity. Or a young woman refusing to compromise her values for popularity. Or a leader who chooses honesty over ambition, empathy over ego.

The modern virtuous woman is not bound by tradition but guided by truth. She does not seek applause, but purpose. She may be educated, ambitious, and fully engaged in public life but she also understands that strength without compassion is hollow, and freedom without responsibility is destructive.

Moreover, the virtuous woman understands that true beauty is internal. While culture often glorifies the external skin-deep beauty, designer labels, and curated personas—the virtuous woman focuses on building something more enduring: character. Her beauty flows from the inside out. It is seen in her choices, her words, her relationships, and the quiet courage with which she faces life's storms.

She also recognizes that virtue is not a static state, but a lifelong journey. It requires daily decisions to choose what is right over what is easy, to speak truth when silence would be safer, and to love when it is simpler to walk away. She is not perfect but she is intentional. And in a world desperate for authenticity, her example speaks louder than any slogan or screen.

As we continue this exploration, let us not idealize the virtuous woman as a distant figure from a forgotten past. She is among us. She is in every woman who leads with love, who chooses sacrifice over selfishness, who lives with purpose rather than pretense. She is not confined to religious or cultural archetypes; she transcends them, reminding us all that virtue is not about being noticed; it is about being rooted.

In the next chapter, we will turn our attention to the contrasting image: the virtual woman. Who is she? What does she represent? And how does her rise challenge or reshape our understanding of what it means to be a woman today?

Devotional:

Proverbs 31:25-26 – "Strength and honour are her clothing... She openeth her mouth with wisdom..."

Romans 12:2 "And be not conformed to this world: but be ye transformed by the renewing of your mind..."

1 Peter 3:3-4 "Whose adorning let it not be that outward adorning... But let it be the hidden man of the heart..."

Chapter 1 The Virtuous Woman

Chapter 2

The Virtual Woman

In contrast to the virtuous woman, the virtual woman is a product of the digital age, existing primarily in the virtual world of the internet and social media. The virtual woman is often characterized by her carefully curated online persona, which may or may not reflect her true self. She may use social media to present a highly stylized and idealized image of herself—one that is designed to impress, attract attention, and fit within the algorithms of online approval.

This version of womanhood is not born in quiet reflection or deep character formation, but rather in rapid response to the demands of an ever-scrolling audience. The virtual woman's identity is sometimes subtly, sometimes overtly shaped by likes, comments, followers, filters, trends, and viral content. She is always online, always visible, and often expected to perform a version of herself that is more appealing than authentic.

That's not to say the virtual woman is inherently fake or shallow. Many women use digital platforms to share meaningful stories, build businesses, advocate for justice, or create communities of support. Technology, in this way, has empowered women like never before, giving them global reach and influence. But with that visibility comes a new set of pressures that can chip away at authenticity and inner peace if not navigated wisely.

Topic: Moral strength, integrity, and spiritual character.

Proverbs 31:25-26 "Strength and honour are her clothing... She openeth her mouth with wisdom..."

Titus 2:3-5 "...that they may teach the young women to be sober, to love their husbands, to love their children..."

Galatians 5:22-23 "But the fruit of the Spirit is love, joy, peace, longsuffering..."

The danger lies in the temptation to replace *being* with *appearing* to prioritize optics over substance, engagement over truth, image over integrity. The virtual woman becomes more about projection than presence. Her digital avatar may be flawless, but her sense of self can easily become fractured, especially when worth is measured by how well she performs online rather than who she is offline.

This performance culture is not exclusive to influencers or celebrities; it has seeped into the daily lives of ordinary women. A young woman posts her "perfect" morning routine, not necessarily because it reflects her everyday life, but because it fits the aesthetic of productivity culture. A mother shares curated family photos while hiding the chaos behind the scenes. A professional woman displays achievements and milestones, subtly pressured to brand herself as "successful" in a way that is palatable and inspiring to others.

The result? A growing disconnect between one's public persona and private reality. This can lead to anxiety, burnout, comparison, and even depression, especially when women feel they are never enough or that they must constantly *edit* themselves to be worthy of attention, affection, or respect.

The virtual woman is also often subjected to intense scrutiny. In the digital world, a woman's value can quickly become tied to how desirable or marketable she is. The lines between empowerment and objectification are increasingly blurred. While some claim ownership over their image as a form of liberation, others are trapped in a cycle of performance that reinforces harmful stereotypes. Beauty becomes currency, and the pressure to maintain a flawless appearance can be relentless.

This hyper-visual culture also influences how women view themselves. Constant exposure to filtered perfection and curated lifestyles can create unrealistic expectations. The virtual woman might feel compelled to compare her real life to someone else's highlight reel, leading to feelings of inadequacy, envy, or even shame.

At the same time, the virtual woman must contend with the erosion of privacy. Her life becomes content. Her joy becomes engagement. Her pain can be turned into a performance. This is not entirely her fault. The digital economy thrives on attention, and social media platforms are designed to reward visibility, not necessarily virtue. But the impact on women's mental and emotional well-being cannot be ignored.

Furthermore, the virtual woman is often fragmented. She may have one version of herself for Instagram, another for LinkedIn, and yet another for family or faith communities. This fragmentation can cause a slow but steady erosion of the true self, making it difficult for women to know who they really are apart from the digital gaze.

Despite all this, we must acknowledge that the virtual woman is not an enemy to be condemned, but a reflection of the times we live in, and she is a woman navigating a complex, digital landscape where identity is constantly negotiated. She is not lacking in intelligence, ambition, or creativity. In fact, many virtual women are incredibly innovative, using digital tools to shape culture, challenge injustice, and redefine modern womanhood. But she is often weary, disconnected, and chasing something she can't quite name.

The challenge, then, is not to reject the virtual world, but to bring *virtue* into it.

What would it look like if the virtual woman reclaimed her sense of self, not through curated perfection, but through honest storytelling and intentional living? What if digital spaces became places of connection, not comparison? What if women used technology to build one another up, rather than measure themselves against each other?

To become more than a digital façade, the virtual

woman must ground her identity in something deeper than the screen. She must cultivate inner character even when no one is watching. She must dare to be authentic in a world that rewards imitation. And she must remember that her worth does not depend on numbers, trends, or validation from strangers online.

Ultimately, the virtual woman is not separate from the virtuous woman; they can coexist. A woman can have an online presence and still be deeply grounded in purpose and values. She can navigate the digital world without losing her soul. But it takes intention, courage, and wisdom.

In the next chapter, we will examine the tensions and potential harmony between these two identities. Can a virtuous woman thrive in a virtual world? Can technology serve, rather than undermine, her journey toward authenticity? And what practices can help women reclaim their true selves in a world that is constantly trying to redefine them?

Topic: Image-focused identity and curated personas.

2 Timothy 3:1-5 "...lovers of their own selves, covetous, boasters... having a form of godliness, but denying the power thereof..."

Matthew 6:1 "Take heed that ye do not your alms before men, to be seen of them..."

Proverbs 31:30 "Favour is deceitful, and beauty is vain: but a woman that feareth the Lord, she shall be praised."

Chapter 2 The Virtual Woman

Let us explore the crossroads where virtue and virtuality meet.

Chapter 3

Characteristics of the Virtuous and Virtual Woman

The differences between the virtuous woman and the virtual woman are not just philosophical; they are deeply practical, manifesting in everyday choices, habits, and how women show up in the world. These two archetypes, while not mutually exclusive, represent contrasting value systems and approaches to identity, purpose, and visibility.

Let us examine the defining characteristics of each. **1 Samuel 16:7** "...for man looketh on the outward appearance, but the Lord looketh on the heart."

James 3:13 "Who is a wise man and endued with knowledge among you? let him shew out of a good conversation his works with meekness of wisdom."

Matthew 23:27-28 "...ye are like unto whited sepulchres, which indeed appear beautiful outward, but are within full of dead men's bones..."

The Virtuous Woman: Strength in the Unseen

The *virtuous woman* is first and foremost defined by her inner life. Her identity is not based on what she does or how she appears, but on who she is at the core. She embodies integrity, meaning that her actions align with her values even when no one is watching. Her honesty is not situational; her compassion is not performative. It is who she is.

Among her most powerful qualities is wisdom, the ability to discern, reflect, and make sound decisions that benefit not just herself but those around her. She does not rush to speak, to prove, or to dominate. Her words carry weight because they are rooted in truth and love. She is often sought for counsel, not because she is loud, but because she is *wise*.

Empathy is another hallmark of the virtuous woman. She listens deeply. She makes space for others. Her emotional intelligence allows her to connect on a human level, and her *selflessness* does not mean she is a doormat. It means she lives in service of something greater than herself: family, community, faith, or purpose. Her power lies in her humility and consistency.

And yet, for all her inner strength, the virtuous woman has often been overlooked in modern culture. In a world that equates visibility with value, the quiet strength of the virtuous woman can seem invisible. But visibility, for her, is not the goal. Her legacy is not measured by views or followers, but by the lives she touches, the trust she builds, and the peace she carries.

That said, **visibility** is not inherently incompatible

with virtue.

A truly virtuous woman can, and sometimes must, be visible. She may lead movements, speak on platforms, or influence others in public spaces. The difference lies in her *motivation*. She is not driven by ego or applause, but by the desire to serve, to uplift, and to be a light in the world. Her presence is not about performance; it is about purpose. She understands that *how* she is seen matters just as much as *being* seen.

In this way, the virtuous woman is not confined to the background. She can take center stage, but she does so with grace, humility, and intentionality.

The Virtual Woman: Power in the Seen

On the other hand, the *virtual woman* is primarily shaped by external perception. She lives in the age of social media, digital platforms, and constant exposure. Her identity is often curated and built around images, captions, content, and engagement. She is not necessarily shallow or insincere, but her energy is often directed outward, toward how she is received by others.

Visibility, for the virtual woman, is not just a byproduct of her life it is often the currency of her identity. In many cases, her value is measured in likes, comments, shares, and followers. These metrics can become the mirror through which she sees herself.

This can lead to both *empowerment* and *distortion*.

Chapter 3 Characteristics of the Virtuous and Virtual

On one hand, visibility has allowed many women to build careers, share important stories, challenge societal norms, and connect across boundaries. The virtual space has provided a voice to the voiceless and a platform for those once marginalized. In this way, the virtual woman can be bold, creative, and revolutionary.

On the other hand, the emphasis on *performance* can create a fragile sense of self. The virtual woman may feel pressure to always be "on" to be beautiful, successful, likable, or relevant. Her image becomes a product, and her presence online is subject to constant evaluation. Authenticity may be sacrificed for aesthetics. Vulnerability may be withheld out of fear of judgment.

Moreover, the virtual woman often lives with a dual consciousness she must both *experience* and *document*. This can lead to disconnection from the present moment and from her own soul: her mind, her will, and her emotions.

Her **visibility** is high, but her *intimacy* with herself may be low.

She might be praised for her appearance, her branding, or her lifestyle, but struggle privately with impostor syndrome, exhaustion, or a lack of deeper connection. She is admired for what she shows but not always known for who she is.

Where Virtue and Virtuality Intersect

These two portraits of the virtuous and the virtual are not meant to polarize women, but to reveal a deeper truth: in every woman exists the tension between being *seen* and being *real*.

The modern woman is navigating both spheres. She may be active online, but still yearns for groundedness. She may have a public platform, but desires a private, meaningful life. She may post selfies, but also wrestle with questions of purpose and integrity.

The key is to recognize the cost of chasing visibility without virtue and to understand the power of bringing *virtue* into *visibility*.

A woman can use her online presence to inspire, educate, or uplift, but it must be rooted in who she truly is. Her content can reflect her convictions. Her image can be a tool for good, not a mask for approval. She can be both virtuous and visible, *but only if she remains true to herself.*

Conclusion: Choosing Depth Over Display

Ultimately, the choice every woman must make is not whether to be virtuous or virtual, but whether her *virtual presence* is aligned with her *inner virtue*. Is what she shows a reflection of who she is? Does her visibility lead to connection or comparison? Is she being shaped more by algorithms or by values?

Chapter 3 Characteristics of the Virtuous and Virtual

In a culture that constantly urges women to be seen, the most radical act may be to *be whole* to cultivate the quiet power of character, and let *that* be what shines.

In the next chapter, we will explore how these two identities often collide and how women can bridge the gap between the expectations of the online world and the truth of their inner selves.

Chapter 4

Differences Between the Virtuous and Virtual
Woman

While the *virtuous woman* and the *virtual woman*
may seem similar at first glance, both may be strong,
influential, and admired; there are important and often
subtle differences that set them apart. These differences
are not merely in lifestyle or personality, but in the
motivations, *values*, and *sources of identity* that guide
them.

Topic: Comparison of motivations, identity, and
values.

Galatians 1:10 – "For do I now persuade men, or
God? or do I seek to please men? for if I yet pleased
men, I should not be the servant of Christ."

Colossians 3:23-24 "And whatsoever ye do, do it
heartily, as to the Lord, and not unto men..."

Matthew 6:21 "For where your treasure is, there will
your heart be also."

Both women may live in the same world. Both may use similar tools. They may even share goals such as influence, success, or connection. But the **heart behind their actions**, and the **outcome of their lives**, reveal distinct paths, one rooted in depth, the other in display.

Source of Identity: Inner Worth vs. Outer Image

The **virtuous woman** is grounded in her *inner life*. Her sense of worth is not dependent on external validation or public perception. She knows who she is, and she draws confidence from her values, her integrity, and her relationship with the divine or her deeper purpose. She doesn't need constant affirmation because she lives from a place of self-awareness and inner peace.

The **virtual woman**, by contrast, often builds her identity through the eyes of others. Her self-worth may rise or fall based on how many people view, like, or comment on her posts. She may feel pressure to maintain a particular image, not necessarily because it reflects her truth, but because it gains attention or approval. In extreme cases, she may become disconnected from her authentic self, losing sight of who she is apart from her digital presence.

This doesn't make the virtual woman shallow; it makes her human. In a world where visibility

is rewarded and anonymity is ignored, many women feel they *must* perform in order to belong. But this constant performance can quietly erode identity, leaving a hollow version of the self that looks beautiful on the outside but feels lost on the inside.

Motivation: Service vs. Validation

At the core of the **virtuous woman** is a heart for service. She is others-centered, not because she lacks ambition or confidence, but because her strength is expressed in generosity, compassion, and meaningful connection. She is fulfilled not by applause, but by the quiet impact she makes on others' lives. She gives without broadcasting. She loves without condition. She leads with humility.

The **virtual woman**, however, is often motivated consciously or not by the pursuit of **attention,**

affirmation, or validation. The digital world has taught her that visibility equals value, so she adapts. She may craft her image, message, or presence in a way that is designed to be *liked* rather than to be *true*. Her focus is often inward: How do I look? What will people think? How can I stay relevant?

This is not always selfish; it is often survival. Women are rewarded for being seen, praised for their aesthetic, and followed for their charisma. But over time, this can lead to a pattern where external validation replaces internal conviction. Instead of asking, "Is this the right thing?" or "Does this align with my values?" she may ask, "Will this go viral?" or "Will this make me more popular?"

The virtuous woman's actions are guided by timeless principles; the virtual woman's by shifting algorithms.

Character vs. Curation

A key difference lies in **consistency**. The virtuous woman strives to live with consistency between her private and public selves. She is not perfect, but she is *authentic*. What she says aligns with how she lives. She makes mistakes, owns them, and grows. Her life may not be glamorous, but it is *real*.

The virtual woman, however, may rely heavily on **curation,** selecting and presenting only the most polished parts of her life. Her presence may be strategically edited, filtered, and posed. There's often a gap between what's projected and what's true. Over time, this can create a dissonance not only for others but for herself, as she begins to feel like a performer in her own life.

Curation isn't inherently bad; it can be creative, empowering, and purposeful. But when curation becomes a mask rather than a mirror, the soul begins to suffer.

Longevity vs. Trendiness

The virtuous woman lives for **legacy**. She is building something that lasts—trust, faith, wisdom, community. Her impact is measured not in fleeting trends but in lasting transformation. She plants seeds that may take years to grow, yet she does so patiently, knowing that true influence is often slow and silent.

The virtual woman often feels the pressure to stay on trend, to post often, to react quickly, to stay relevant. Her influence can be widespread but shallow, quickly rising and just as quickly forgotten. Because digital culture moves so fast, she may struggle to pause, reflect, or root herself in anything lasting. She is always updating, always adapting, always moving.

While the virtuous woman embraces **depth**, the virtual woman is often consumed by **speed**.

Relationship with Visibility

Perhaps the most telling difference between the two lies in how each woman relates to **visibility**. The virtuous woman may be visible, but she does not seek visibility for its own sake. Her goal is not to be seen, but to *see clearly, to see* truth, to see others, and to see herself with grace and honesty. If she is recognized, she uses that platform to serve others. If she is not, she remains faithful.

The virtual woman often lives *for* visibility. To be unseen is to feel unimportant. She may fear invisibility more than irrelevance. Her energy is directed toward staying visible even if it means compromising her values or stretching her truth.

Conclusion: A Matter of the Heart

At the end of the day, the difference between the virtuous and virtual woman is not in what they do, but in *why* they do it and *who* they are becoming in the process.

The virtuous woman builds her life on unshakable principles.

The virtual woman builds her brand on shifting expectations.

The virtuous woman lives from the inside out.

The virtual woman lives from the outside in.

And yet, in today's world, many women are caught somewhere in the middle.

The goal is not to shame the virtual woman or idealize

the virtuous woman; it is to recognize where we are and choose with intention who we want to become.

We must ask: **What defines me? Who am I when no one is watching? Is my life shaped by truth or by trends?**

Chapter 5

The Challenges of Modern Womanhood

In today's world, women face a unique and often overwhelming set of challenges as they strive to balance the demands of modern life with traditional expectations of femininity, morality, and personal identity. While previous generations may have struggled primarily with societal roles defined by family, religion, and community, today's woman must also contend with the ever-present pressures of a hyperconnected, hyper-visual digital culture.

Topic: The collision of traditional values with modern pressures.

Ecclesiastes 1:8-9 "All things are full of labour; man cannot utter it... There is no new thing under the sun."

Isaiah 5:20 "Woe unto them that call evil good, and good evil..."

Philippians 4:8 "...whatsoever things are true... whatsoever things are pure... think on these things."

Chapter 5 The Challenges of Modern Womanhood

This is the age of the *collision*—where the **virtuous woman** and the **virtual woman** meet, clash, and often blur.

The **virtuous woman**, rooted in timeless values such as integrity, humility, faith, service, and compassion, still represents an ideal for many. Whether shaped by religious tradition, cultural heritage, or personal conviction, her compass is internal. She aspires to live a life of meaning and character, to build strong relationships, to contribute to her family or community, and to grow spiritually and emotionally.

But the **virtual world** and its creation, the *virtual woman,* presents a different vision of success and womanhood. Online, women are often celebrated for their beauty, visibility, branding, and ability to stay relevant in a rapidly evolving digital space. Social media platforms reward curated perfection, instant gratification, and performance-driven content. In this world, to be *seen* is often more valuable than to be *real*.

For many women, this creates a profound tension: **How can I live authentically when I feel pressure to perform? How can I be virtuous when virtual values dominate the culture around me?**

The Double Life: When Values and Visibility Collide

The modern woman often feels torn between two worlds. She may believe in modesty, but feels pressured to dress for likes. She may value humility, but feel compelled to self-promote. She may long for deep relationships, but find herself trapped in superficial online interactions.

This internal conflict is not just psychological; it's spiritual, emotional, and even physical. It's the quiet ache of knowing you are not living fully aligned with who you truly are. It's the fatigue that comes from switching between masks. It's the guilt of being applauded online while feeling disconnected offline. It's the anxiety of wondering if the *real you* is enough without the filters, edits, or audience.

This *collision of identities* is one of the defining struggles of modern womanhood.

On one side: a longing for substance, rootedness, and virtue.
On the other: the ever-present demand to be polished, appealing, and constantly *visible*.

The pressure is amplified by the **sheer accessibility of visibility**. Any woman with a smartphone can craft a persona, build a brand, or go viral. While this presents incredible opportunities, especially for marginalized voices, it also raises the stakes for comparison, competition, and personal compromise, and the cost is high.

Mental and Emotional Burnout

Women today are reporting record levels of burnout, anxiety, and depression. Much of this is fueled not just by work or family demands, but by the *emotional labor* of maintaining a public self. Social media requires constant updates, engagement, and vigilance. Even moments of joy, vacations, birthdays, and achievements are rarely just for personal celebration. They must be *documented*, captioned, and shared.

This creates a performative rhythm of life, where women are not simply *living*, but constantly *staging* their lives for public consumption.

The result? Exhaustion. Disconnection. A loss of authenticity.

Women begin to question: Who am I *really*, when no one is watching? Am I becoming the woman I *appear* to be, or am I slowly losing the one I was meant to become?

Cultural Confusion: Mixed Messages About Femininity

Another layer of complexity comes from **conflicting cultural messages**. In one moment, women are encouraged to embrace traditional roles of being nurturing, modest, and family-centered. In the next, they are told to be fierce, independent, sensual, and unapologetically bold. The virtuous woman is still upheld in many faith communities, yet mainstream culture often mocks her as naive, outdated, or weak.

At the same time, the virtual woman is celebrated *but only if she meets certain standards*. Be visible, but not too vulnerable. Be sexy, but not too sexual. Be successful, but still likable. Be confident, but not intimidating.

These contradictions leave many women walking a tightrope, constantly adjusting who they are based on where they are and who's watching.

The result? Identity fragmentation, moral fatigue, and confusion about what it really means to be a "good woman."

The Loss of Sacred Space

Perhaps the greatest casualty in the collision between the virtuous and virtual woman is the **loss of sacred space, the** quiet, hidden places where character is formed, where virtue is nurtured, and where the soul is restored.

Digital life is noisy, fast, and distracting. It leaves little room for solitude, contemplation, prayer, or stillness, all of which are essential for cultivating inner strength and clarity. The virtuous woman thrives in these sacred spaces. She draws power from silence. She listens deeply to her conscience. She invests in the invisible work of becoming.

But when life becomes a constant performance, these spaces disappear. Women are left spiritually malnourished, visibly active, but inwardly depleted.

The Path Forward: Integration, Not Isolation

So what is the way forward?

It is not to reject the digital world or romanticize the past. Nor is it to surrender to the virtual mold and abandon virtue altogether. The answer lies in **integration** of the inner life into the outer world, allowing character to inform content, and choosing to live with wholeness rather than fragmentation.

Chapter 5 The Challenges of Modern Womanhood

This begins by asking hard questions:

Is my online persona aligned with who I am when no one is watching?

Am I using visibility to serve others, or to seek validation?

What does success look like for me based on *my* values, not the world's?

Am I becoming more virtuous, or just more visible?

Women who begin to live with this kind of intentionality reclaim their power, not the power of performance, but the power of *presence*. They show up authentically. They choose purpose over popularity. They let their inner life lead their outer expression.

And in doing so, they show the world that **virtue is not obsolete; it is** radical, beautiful, and deeply needed in this age.

Chapter 6

Virtue and Virtuality – Bridging the Divide

The **virtuous woman** and the **virtual woman** represent two distinct approaches to womanhood in the 21st Century, each shaped by different influences, values, and cultural expectations. Yet they are not merely opposing archetypes; they are reflections of a deeper inner struggle that many modern women face: *the tension between being true to oneself and being accepted by the world.*

The **virtuous woman** embodies timeless qualities of kindness**, compassion, wisdom, humility, faithfulness, and selflessness**. She is not perfect, but she is grounded. Her beauty radiates from within. Her strength lies in her ability to endure, nurture, uplift, and walk in truth regardless of the cultural tides. She builds her life on the foundation of character, not applause. She lives for legacy, not for likes.

The **virtual woman**, on the other hand, is often shaped by a world that values **image over substance** and **visibility over virtue**. She carefully curates her appearance and digital presence to fit into a culture that demands perfection, influence, and instant gratification. She may not be inherently vain or shallow, but her environment constantly rewards her for *how she looks* and *how she performs*, not *who she is*.

And so, the modern woman lives in the **collision zone** between these two forces. She is pulled in one direction by her longing for authenticity and purpose, and in the other by the pressure to remain seen, praised, and relevant. This constant back-and-forth can feel exhausting, confusing, and even soul-crushing.

The Dangers of Extremes

To choose only one path to live *entirely* as the virtuous woman or *entirely* as the virtual woman can lead to imbalance.

A woman who clings solely to traditional values without understanding or engaging the world around her may feel disconnected, irrelevant, or unheard. She may begin to hide her voice out of fear of being misunderstood. Her inner richness may go unseen because she avoids platforms that could amplify her message.

On the other hand, a woman who lives only through her virtual image may become consumed by the need for constant validation. Her sense of worth may become fragile, rising and falling with every click, comment, and view. Over time, her true self may begin to fade beneath the persona she has created to survive or succeed.

Neither extreme allows a woman to flourish.

Wholeness comes from balance.

Embracing a New Vision: Wholeness Over Performance

To be a good woman in the modern world is not to choose between being virtuous and being visible. It is to embrace **wholeness** to live with integrity both *online* and *offline*, to cultivate both *inner character* and *outer beauty*, to be both *real* and *refined*.

A truly whole woman doesn't have to hide her strength or silence her voice to be considered virtuous. She doesn't have to chase digital fame to feel validated. She recognizes that she can be both influential and authentic, both present in the world and rooted in her values.

This is the woman who lives from the **inside out**. She shows up online as the same woman she is in private. She is intentional about her visibility, using it not to impress, but to *inspire*. She doesn't reject technology, but she doesn't let it define her either. She wears her identity with confidence, not because it's flawless, but because it's *true*.

She strives for **both inner and outer beauty**, understanding that these are not opposites, but partners when properly aligned. Her physical presence reflects her inner dignity. Her words uplift, her actions serve, and her presence leaves others better than she found them.

The Invitation to Today's Woman

In a world full of contradictions, women are being

called to rise not by choosing performance over principle, or principle over presence, but by *bridging the two.*

This is not easy. It requires discernment, discipline, and courage. It means asking the hard questions:

Am I living for likes or for legacy?

Does my online presence reflect my true character?

Am I cultivating who I am, or only curating what I seem to be?

Do I want to be praised or to be *known, trusted,* and *respected?*

Each woman must answer these questions for herself. But the truth remains: A life built on virtue will *always outlast* a life built on vanity.

A Final Word of Hope

The beauty of womanhood today is that **you do not have to choose between being strong and being seen, between being virtuous and being relevant.** You are allowed to evolve, to grow, to learn from mistakes, and to reclaim your true self even if you've lost her for a while in the noise of the world.

This book has not been written to condemn, but to **call** women back to themselves. To remind them that who they are in the quiet is more important than who they are in the spotlight. To affirm that **true virtue is never outdated**, and that real influence begins with *being* *whole.*

As we step forward into the final chapter, the question is not just *Who do I want to be seen as?* But rather, *Who am I becoming?*

Micah 6:8 – "He hath shewed thee, O man, what is good... to do justly, and to love mercy, and to walk humbly with thy God."

Proverbs 4:23 "Keep thy heart with all diligence; for out of it are the issues of life."

Psalm 139:23-24 "Search me, O God, and know my heart... and lead me in the way everlasting."

Chapter 7

Reclaiming Virtue in a Virtual World

We live in a time where the virtual world is not just part of our lives, it *shapes* our lives. From the moment we wake up, we are surrounded by screens, social media feeds, online opinions, and digital performance. Our worth is often measured in followers, likes, and curated appearances. In this world, **virtue** can feel outdated, invisible, or even irrelevant.

But virtue is not gone; it is simply waiting to be *reclaimed*.

Reclaiming virtue in a virtual world does not mean abandoning the digital space. It does not mean living in silence or rejecting modern technology. Rather, it means learning how to **live by truth**, **walk in wisdom**, and **stay grounded in character**, even as the world demands constant performance.

It means choosing authenticity over appearance, purpose over popularity, and wholeness over hype.

Chapter 7 Reclaiming Virtue in a Virtual World

Understanding What Virtue Truly Is

Before we can reclaim virtue, we must understand it. Virtue is not a personality type, a dress code, or a social role—it is the embodiment of **moral strength**, **spiritual integrity**, and **inner beauty**. It includes qualities like:

Kindness – not weakness, but strength under control.

Self-control – resisting the need for instant validation.

Wisdom – seeing beyond the moment and living with intention.

Faithfulness – to God, to others, and to one's true self.

Humility – knowing who you are without needing to prove it.

Virtue is not loud. It is not flashy. It does not trend or go viral. But it is *powerful*, and it changes the world one heart, one home, one woman at a time.

Recognizing the Pull of the Virtual Self

The virtual self thrives on attention. It tells us we must always be "on." Always visible. Always performing. It whispers that if we're not seen, we don't matter.

But here is the truth: **Visibility is not the same as value.**

To reclaim virtue, we must confront the virtual self and recognize the lies we've believed:

That we are only as good as our appearance.

That our influence is measured in numbers.

That we must compare ourselves to others to know our worth.

The first step to reclaiming virtue is to *disentangle our identity* from our online image. This doesn't mean deleting social media; it means **no longer depending on it for meaning**.

Ask yourself: Who am I when the cameras are off? Who am I when no one is watching?

That is where virtue begins.

Cultivating the Hidden Life

In Scripture, much is said about the power of the *hidden life, the* life lived in private, where character is formed. This life is not always seen, but it is where the roots of virtue grow deep.

Set aside time for silence. Reflection is where clarity is born.

Pray and seek wisdom. A woman grounded in God's Word is not easily shaken.

Journal your thoughts and values. Writing helps you stay anchored in truth.

Do good in secret. When we serve without applause, our motives are purified.

The virtual world trains us to live for visibility. But the *virtuous woman* finds power in the quiet because she knows that true beauty is not built in the spotlight, but in the **secret places** of the soul.

Using the Virtual Space with Virtue

Reclaiming virtue doesn't require abandoning virtual space. In fact, it means **redeeming it**.

You can be both virtuous and visible, but your *why* must change.

Use your voice to uplift. Share wisdom, not just aesthetics.

Show your real life, not just your highlight reel. Vulnerability invites connection.

Model grace in conflict. The world notices when a woman refuses to gossip, shame, or retaliate.

Encourage others to live from a place of wholeness. Be a light in the digital world, not just another echo of the culture.

Ask: Am I reflecting the world, or transforming it?

The goal is not perfection, it is presence. *A woman who is fully present in her values, her faith, and her identity will always shine even on the smallest screen.*

Building Relationships that Strengthen Virtue

One of the greatest dangers of the virtual world is

isolation. We are surrounded by people online, yet deeply alone. We connect digitally but rarely grow spiritually.

To reclaim virtue, surround yourself with people who help you:

Stay accountable to your values.

Encourage truth, not trends.

Challenge you to go deeper.

Remind you who you really are.

Mentorship, sisterhood, and faith-based communities, these relationships are essential to virtue. The virtual world moves fast. You need people who will help you slow down and stay grounded.

Forgiving Yourself and Starting Fresh

Some women feel they've gone too far into virtual life. Too much performance. Too much compromise. Too many masks.

But here is the good news: **You are not too far gone.**

Reclaiming virtue is not about having a perfect past; it's about choosing a new path today.

You can begin again.
You can re-center your life.
You can choose to be the woman you were always meant to be: strong, kind, wise, gracious, and whole.

Every act of honesty, every step of integrity, every word of love, it all counts. It all heals. It all restores.

You don't have to become invisible to reclaim virtue. You simply have to become **authentic**.

In Closing: A Better Way Forward

The world doesn't need more perfection.
It needs more *presence*.
It needs more women who are real, rooted, and rising.
Women who live from the inside out.
Women who walk in truth in a world obsessed with image.
Women who know that beauty begins in the soul.

To reclaim virtue in a virtual world is to say:

"I will not be defined by the algorithm. I will be defined by my *character*."

It is to believe that **true influence starts with integrity**.

It is to live a life so aligned with your values that no platform, no trend, no crowd can shake you.

This is what it means to be whole.
This is what it means to be free.
This is what it means to be *virtuous* in a virtual world.

Topic: Six thoughts for living virtuously with purpose, integrity, and authenticity in a digitally driven world.

1. Understanding What Virtue Truly Is

- **Proverbs 31:10**
  "Who can find a virtuous woman? for her price is far above rubies."

- **Philippians 4:8**
  "Finally, brethren, whatsoever things are true, whatsoever things are honest, whatsoever things are just... if there be any virtue, and if there be any praise, think on these things."

- **Galatians 5:22-23**
  "But the fruit of the Spirit is love, joy, peace, longsuffering, gentleness, goodness, faith, Meekness, temperance: against such there is no law."

2. Recognizing the Pull of the Virtual Self

- **Romans 12:2**
  "And be not conformed to this world: but be ye transformed by the renewing of your mind..."

- **Matthew 6:1**
  "Take heed that ye do not your alms before men, to be seen of them..."

- **1 John 2:15-16**
  "Love not the world, neither the things that are in the world... the lust of the flesh, and the lust of the eyes, and the pride of life, is not of the Father..."

3. Cultivating the Hidden Life

- **Matthew 6:6**
  "But thou, when thou prayest, enter into thy closet, and when thou hast shut thy door, pray to thy Father which is in secret..."

- **Colossians 3:3**
  "For ye are dead, and your life is hid with Christ in God."

- **Psalm 91:1**
  "He that dwelleth in the secret place of the most High shall abide under the shadow of the Almighty."

4. Using Virtual Space with Virtue

- **Proverbs 15:2**
  "The tongue of the wise useth knowledge aright: but the mouth of fools poureth out foolishness."

- **Ephesians 4:29**
  "Let no corrupt communication proceed out of your mouth, but that which is good to the use of edifying..."

- **Matthew 5:14-16**
  "Ye are the light of the world... Let your light so shine before men, that they may see your good works, and glorify your Father which is in heaven."

5. Building Relationships That Strengthen Virtue

- **Proverbs 27:17**
  "Iron sharpeneth iron; so a man sharpeneth the countenance of his friend."

- **Ecclesiastes 4:9-10**
  "Two are better than one... For if they fall, the one will lift up his fellow..."

- **Hebrews 10:24-25**
  "And let us consider one another to provoke unto love and to good works... exhorting one another..."

6. Forgiving Yourself and Starting Fresh

- **2 Corinthians 5:17**
  "Therefore if any man be in Christ, he is a new creature: old things are passed away; behold, all things are become new."

- **Isaiah 1:18**
  "Come now, and let us reason together, saith the Lord: though your sins be as scarlet, they shall be as white as snow..."

- **Lamentations 3:22-23**
  "It is of the Lord's mercies that we are not consumed... They are new every morning: great is thy faithfulness."

Chapter 8

Raising Virtuous Daughters in a Virtual
Culture

As someone blessed to have granddaughters and adopted daughters woven deeply into my life, I understand firsthand the profound responsibility and privilege it is to help guide young women through the complexities of today's world. The culture they navigate is unlike any before it. The **virtual landscape** shapes much of their identity, social interactions, and sense of self-worth.

Micah 6:8
"He hath shewed thee, O man, what is good; and what doth the Lord require of thee, but to do justly, and to love mercy, and to walk humbly with thy God?"

While technology offers incredible opportunities for learning, connection, and creativity, it also presents unique challenges: unrealistic beauty standards, cyberbullying, the pressure to perform online, and the temptation to equate self-value with social media approval. As mentors, caregivers, and role models, our calling is to help these daughters grow into women who are **grounded in virtue,** women who know their worth beyond the screen and live with courage, integrity, and grace.

Rooting Identity in Something Unshakeable

The first step in raising virtuous daughters in a virtual culture is helping them **root their identity in something unshakeable**, a truth that doesn't change with algorithms, followers, or trends.

Teach them that their true worth is not found in likes or comments but in who they are **created to be:** children of God, made in His image, loved deeply and unconditionally.

Encourage regular engagement with Scripture and prayer, so they grow up hearing and internalizing God's voice above the noise of the world. Help them memorize verses that remind them of their inherent value and purpose, such as:

"I am fearfully and wonderfully made" (Psalm 139:14)

"You are precious in my eyes" (Isaiah 43:4)

"Do not be conformed to this world" (Romans 12:2)

Modeling Virtue Through Your Life

Young women learn far more from what they *see* than what they *hear*. Your life is the most powerful curriculum for teaching virtue.

Demonstrate kindness, honesty, patience, and humility in your daily actions. Show them how to balance technology use with real-life relationships, how to handle conflict gracefully, and how to stand firm in convictions even when the world pulls another way.

Let them see you **choose authenticity over appearance**, vulnerability over perfection, and service over self-promotion.

Teaching Digital Discernment

In a virtual culture, discernment is a crucial skill.

Help your daughters learn to navigate social media and digital spaces with eyes wide open. Teach them to question:

What am I consuming online? Does it build me up or tear me down?

Who am I trying to please with my posts? Myself or others?

How can I protect my heart and mind from harmful influences?

Encourage healthy boundaries: limited screen time, mindful engagement, and regular digital detoxes.

Show them how to curate their online presence with integrity, being honest and uplifting, not chasing approval through superficial means.

Encouraging Courage to Be Different

The virtual world often rewards conformity to fleeting trends, but virtue often requires **courage to be different**.

Empower your daughters to stand firm in their values—even if that means going against the crowd. Celebrate their uniqueness and individuality. Teach them that true strength lies in **being authentic**, not popular.

Remind them that the virtuous woman's path is not always the easiest, but it is the most fulfilling.

Building a Community of Support

No girl grows into virtue in isolation. Surround your daughters with mentors, friends, and faith communities who will:

Encourage their growth

Hold them accountable to their values

Offer wisdom and love in times of challenge

Create safe spaces—whether in your home, church, or social groups where they can express their struggles and victories honestly.

Preparing Them for Leadership

Virtuous daughters grow into women who lead not by force or fame, but by example and influence rooted in character.

Teach them leadership skills grounded in service: empathy, listening, problem-solving, and resilience. Show them how to use their voice for good online and offline.

Encourage their passions and talents and help them see that their influence matters far beyond the virtual world.

A Personal Commitment

Raising virtuous daughters in this virtual age requires prayerful dedication, intentional teaching, and abundant grace for them and for yourself. It is a journey filled with challenges and joys, mistakes and breakthroughs.

But it is one of the most worthwhile investments you can make, not just for the daughters in your life, but for the generations they will influence in turn.

May we all rise to the call of nurturing women of strength, wisdom, and virtue that help women shine their light in a world that desperately needs it.

Scripture References for Chapter 8

"Raising Virtuous Daughters in a Virtual Culture" (KJV)

These verses reinforce the themes of identity, guidance, example, discernment, and spiritual growth for both the daughters and the mentors who shape them.

1. Rooting Identity in Something Unshakeable

Psalm 139:14 – *"I will praise thee; for I am fearfully and wonderfully made..."*

Isaiah 43:4 – *"Since thou wast precious in my sight, thou hast been honourable, and I have loved thee..."*

Romans 12:2 – *"And be not conformed to this world: but be ye transformed by the renewing of your mind..."*

1 Peter 2:9 – *"But ye are a chosen generation, a royal priesthood, an holy nation, a peculiar people..."*

2. Modeling Virtue Through Your Life

Proverbs 22:6 – *"Train up a child in the way he should go: and when he is old, he will not depart from it."*

Titus 2:7 – *"In all things shewing thyself a pattern of good works..."*

Matthew 5:16 – *"Let your light so shine before men, that they may see your good works, and glorify your Father..."*

3. Teaching Digital Discernment

1 Thessalonians 5:21-22 *"Prove all things; hold fast that which is good. Abstain from all appearance of evil."*

Proverbs 4:23 *"Keep thy heart with all diligence; for out of it are the issues of life."*

Philippians 4:8 *"Whatsoever things are true... honest... just... pure... lovely... think on these things."*

4. Encouraging Courage to Be Different

Joshua 1:9 – *"Be strong and of a good courage... for the Lord thy God is with thee..."*

Romans 1:16 – *"For I am not ashamed of the gospel of Christ..."*

Galatians 1:10 – *"Do I seek to please men? for if I yet pleased men, I should not be the servant of Christ."*

5. Building a Community of Support

Ecclesiastes 4:9-10 *"Two are better than one... for if they fall, the one will lift up his fellow..."*

Proverbs 13:20 *"He that walketh with wise men shall be wise..."*

Hebrews 10:24-25 *"...provoke unto love and to good works: Not forsaking the assembling of ourselves together..."*

6. Preparing Them for Leadership

1 Timothy 4:12 *"Let no man despise thy youth; but be thou an example of the believers..."*

Proverbs 31:26 *"She openeth her mouth with wisdom; and in her tongue is the law of kindness."*

Esther 4:14 *"...who knoweth whether thou art come to the kingdom for such a time as this?"*

Appendix

Reflection and Application

Key Questions for Mentors, Mothers, and Grandmothers:

1. **Identity & Purpose**

   o Am I helping the girls in my life see themselves through God's eyes?

   o Do I model where true value comes from God's approval rather than man's?

2. **Digital Influence**

   o How do I talk about and interact with social media in my own life?

   o Do my granddaughters see me choosing peace and privacy over performance?

3. **Spiritual Foundation**

   o Are we praying together?

   o Do we read Scripture, or discuss what virtue looks like in today's world?

4. Emotional Safety

o   Have I created a safe space for them to share struggles without fear of judgment?

o   Am I listening more than lecturing?

5. Legacy

o   What values do I want to leave behind?

o   Am I living them now in a way they can follow?

7 Day Devotional

7 Days to Reclaiming Virtue with the Next
Generation

Each day includes a focus verse, short reflection, and action step. Perfect for journaling or doing together with a daughter, granddaughter, or mentee.

Day 1: God Defines Her Worth

Psalm 139:14
Reflection: She is already enough. Remind her of who she is in God's eyes, not the world's lens.

Action: Write a note or message reminding her of her beauty and value beyond appearances.

Day 2: Model What You Teach

Titus 2:7

Reflection: They watch what you do more than what you say. Your life is your lesson.

Action: Choose one virtuous behavior to practice intentionally today (e.g., patience, generosity).

Day 3: Train Her to Think Critically

Proverbs 4:23

Reflection: Teach her to guard her heart, not close it, but protect it from the wrong influences.

Action: Talk with her about how to decide what's healthy to consume online.

Day 4: She Has Permission to Be Different

Romans 12:2
Reflection: She doesn't need to fit in; she was born to stand out for God's glory.

Action: Share a story from your own life when choosing virtue over popularity paid off.

Day 5: Surround Her With Strength

Ecclesiastes 4:9-10
Reflection: We all need each other. Even strong girls need soft landings.

Action: Introduce her to a woman of faith who inspires you, or set up a girl's group for godly support.

Day 6: She Can Lead With Grace

1 Timothy 4:12
Reflection: Age doesn't disqualify her. God can use her voice now.

Action: Encourage her to take leadership in a small way at church, home, or school.

Day 7: You Were Chosen to Guide Her

Esther 4:14
Reflection: God placed you in her life *on purpose*.

Action: Pray for her by name today. Ask God for wisdom and strength to guide her well.

Dr. Katrina Edwards

SCAN ME

Call or Text:
770-240-0089 Press Extension 1
Web: KLEpub.com
Email Services@klepub.com

It's time to start and finish **YOUR Story**!

KLE Publishing specializes in helping people become authors. In as little as 15 to 90 days, we can help you develop your books and e-books and publish to 39,000 outlets! We also offer audiobook services.

Write, Edit, Format, Publish
We can help from
Start to Finish.

Explore and learn more about published authors affiliated with KLE.

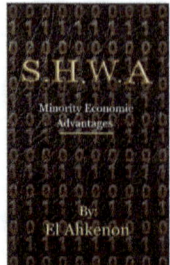  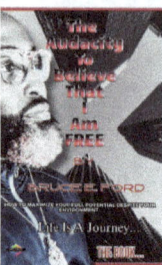  

 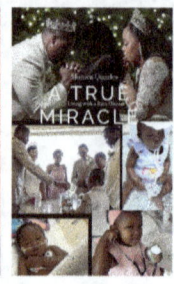   

KLEPub.com